CLASSIC CARS

MotoR Mania

by Jeffrey Zuehlke

Jan Lahtonen, consultant and safety engineer, auto mechanic, and lifelong automobile enthusiast

Lerner Publications Company • Minneapolis

For Gramps, a true classic

Cover Photo: The 1960 Chevrolet Corvette had a powerful engine and was available in eight colors.

Lerner Publications Company
A division of Lerner Publishing Group
241 First Avenue North
Minneapolis, MN 55401 U.S.A.

Website address: www.lernerbooks.com

Library of Congress Cataloging-in-Publication Data

Zuehlke, Jeffrey, 1968–
    Classic cars / by Jeffrey Zuehlke.
      p.   cm. — (Motor mania)
    Includes bibliographical references and index.
    ISBN-13: 978–0–8225–5926–9 (lib. bdg. : alk. paper)
    ISBN-10: 0–8225–5926–9 (lib. bdg. : alk. paper)
    1. Antique and classic cars. I. Title. II. Series.
  TL15.Z84 2007
    629.222—dc22   2006013742

Manufactured in the United States of America
1 2 3 4 5 6 – DP – 12 11 10 09 08 07

Contents

WHAT IS A CLASSIC CAR?

What is a classic car? It's a car that's special for one reason or another. It's a car that's worth keeping for many years. Classic cars are collector's items.

Not everyone agrees on what makes a car a classic. A classic car might be very rare. For example, the Tucker Corporation built only 51 Tucker Torpedoes before going out of business in the late 1940s. These cars are highly prized by collectors.

On the other hand, a classic car might not be rare at all. For example, the famous 1957 Chevrolet Bel Air is the most popular classic U.S. car. Bel Airs are not hard to find. Chevrolet built hundreds of thousands of them.

Most classic cars are beautiful vehicles. They have an appealing look. Yet some cars are classics for just the opposite reason. Take the Ford Motor Company's Edsel line of the late 1950s. Most people think these cars are ugly. But some people like the Edsel because it is unique.

This book is about classic cars from the most exciting time in U.S. automotive history, from the end of World War II (1939–1945) through the 1970s. This was the heyday of U.S. cars. During this time, U.S. automakers built some of the most beautiful and exciting cars the world has ever seen. Some of the cars described here are more popular than others. But all are considered classics.

The 1957 Chevrolet Bel Air might be the greatest American classic car of all time. It first appeared in late 1956. Thousands of Bel Airs can still be found on roads across the country.

Chapter One

CLASSIC CAR HISTORY

During World War II, U.S. automakers switched from making cars to producing supplies for the war. This Chrysler factory made tanks.

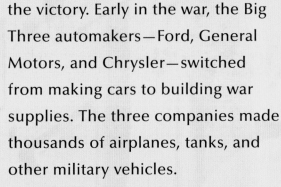

The United States came out of World War II as the richest country on earth. U.S. industry had worked night and day for years making the supplies needed to win the war. U.S. automakers had played a big part in the victory. Early in the war, the Big Three automakers—Ford, General Motors, and Chrysler—switched from making cars to building war supplies. The three companies made thousands of airplanes, tanks, and other military vehicles.

When the war ended in 1945, Americans looked forward to some fun after years of work and hardship. Millions of U.S. soldiers returned home from the war. They had money to spend and were eager to start new lives. Meanwhile, tens of millions of U.S. workers were looking forward to spending the wages they had earned

over the past few years. And what better way to spend money than by buying a new car?

Slowly but Surely

New cars were hard to come by in the first years after the war. Only a handful had been built between 1939 and 1945. And it took U.S. automakers some time to reorganize their factories for making cars again. But within a few years, new cars were rolling off assembly lines at record speeds.

These new and exciting cars were like nothing ever seen before. Cars of the late 1940s were lower, sleeker, and faster than earlier machines. They featured fenders and bodies that blended smoothly together. They were also large and spacious.

By 1947 automakers were producing cars again. Within a few years, production would reach record numbers.

DID YOU KNOW?
Automakers generally take about four years to design and produce a new car model.

The groundbreaking 1949 Ford was one of the first all-new cars produced in the United States after World War II. Its combination of style and power was popular with consumers.

One of the most famous cars of this time was the 1948 Tucker Torpedo. The short-lived Tucker Corporation built only 51 of these machines before going out of business. The Torpedo featured several new features. One was a center headlight that swiveled as the car turned. Another was an un-crushable passenger box and a padded dashboard. These features protected people inside the car during an accident. The low, streamlined Tucker also had a big, powerful engine. It had a

top speed of 120 miles (193 kilometers) per hour—very fast for the time.

The first big group of great postwar cars arrived with the 1949 model year. One of the biggest hits of that year was the 1949 Ford. This car had a smooth, rounded look and a uniquely shaped grille. The round center of the grille looked like a bullet flying out of the front of the car. The 1949 Ford also came with a powerful V8 engine. (A V8 engine has eight cylinders arranged in the shape of a V.) The car was nice to look at and fun to drive. Ford sold more than one million of them.

Meanwhile, Chrysler's Town and Country featured a popular style of this period. The car's trunk, doors, and side panels were made of polished wood. Ford and General Motors (GM) offered their own woodies during these years.

Like many GM cars, the 1949 Buick Roadmaster and Cadillac Series 62 shared the same body shape. Each car had a long, straight hood and a roof that gently sloped down to the rear. (This rear body style is known as a fastback.) The differences between the cars were in the details. The Roadmaster featured a gleaming 25-slat front grille and engine-cooling ventiports on the front fenders.

The Cadillac Series 62's most unique features were two bumps on its rear fenders. Harley Earl, GM's chief of design, came up with these tail fins. Earl got the idea from the twin tails of the P-38 Lightning, a World War II fighter plane. Later, tail fins became all the rage in automobile design.

Harley Earl

Harley Earl (1893–1969) *(right)* is the most famous automobile designer in U.S. history. Working for GM from 1927 to 1959, his design team created some of the greatest classic cars of all time. They include the Corvette and the famous Cadillacs from the years after World War II. Earl introduced many car design changes, such as chrome trim, two-tone paint jobs, wraparound windshields, and tail fins.

Earl also pioneered the concept car idea. He created exciting automobiles that hinted at what future GM cars might look like. Then he toured the country with the cars to see what the public thought of them. Concept cars that were a hit with the public were considered for mass production.

The 1950s: The Golden Age of U.S. Cars

By this time, GM, Chrysler, and Ford had latched on to an idea to sell more cars. Each year automakers made changes and improvements to their cars. This made the older cars seem a bit out of date, or obsolete. The changes fed the public's hunger for newer and better cars. Some of these changes were small. For example, new models might have different trim or a new style of grille. Other changes were major redesigns that resulted in cars that were nearly all new.

Harley Earl's design team dreamed up a fleet of classic machines for GM

Many cars of the 1950s were large, bulky machines. The 1953 Corvette broke that mold with its light-weight body and sporty look.

in the early 1950s. GM's luxury division, Cadillac, led the way. Cadillac produced a line of shapely cars with lots of gleaming chrome trim. Pointed bumpers, chrome accents, and tail fins were the trend. These cars were big and heavy. They had powerful engines and lots of room for passengers.

But not all GM cars stuck to this idea. In 1953 GM's Chevrolet division introduced the Corvette. This was a small, sporty two-door coupe. The exciting little machine looked like a European-style race car. The Corvette had a body made of lightweight fiberglass. For some, the Corvette was a welcome change from the bigger machines of the time.

Chrysler and Ford worked hard to keep up with GM. Ford introduced its own sports car in 1955, the Thunderbird. Chrysler launched redesigns for its Chrysler, Plymouth, Dodge, and DeSoto lines. (The DeSoto division was dropped a few

years later.) The company called its new line the $100 Million Look, after the huge amount of money it spent to develop the cars.

One of the most famous of these cars is the 1955 Chrysler C-300. This was a big luxury sedan. It was fitted with a powerful engine called the Firepower Hemi V8. The 300 stood for the amount of horsepower the engine produced. (Horsepower is a unit used to measure an engine's power.) Most cars of the time produced about 150 to 200 horsepower. The C-300 was one of the fastest cars on the road. It could reach 130 miles (209 km) per hour.

The 1955 Chrysler C-300 was one of the fastest cars on the road when it was produced. It could go from 0 to 60 miles (96 km) per hour in about 10 seconds.

How an Internal Combustion Engine Works

Internal combustion engines create power by burning a mixture of fuel and air *(right)*. Most small or midsized cars have four- or six-cylinder engines that produce less horsepower—between 100 to 200 horsepower. But a big V8 can produce 300, 400, or more horsepower. More horsepower means more speed.

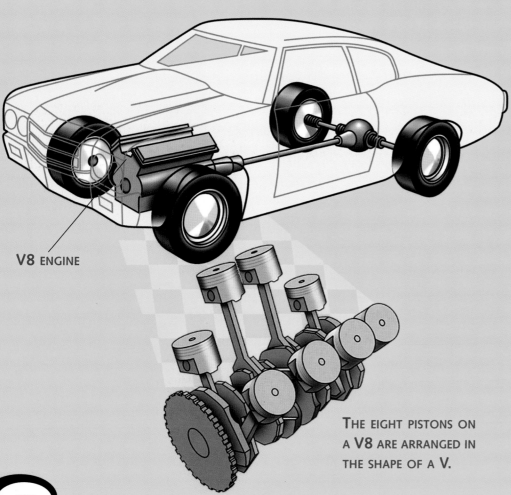

V8 ENGINE

THE EIGHT PISTONS ON A V8 ARE ARRANGED IN THE SHAPE OF A V.

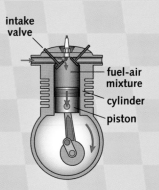

1. INTAKE STROKE
The piston moves down the cylinder and draws the fuel-air mixture into the cylinder through the intake valve.

intake valve
fuel-air mixture
cylinder
piston

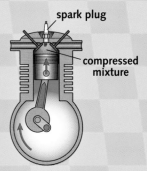

2. COMPRESSION STROKE
The piston moves up and compresses the fuel-air mixture. The spark plug ignites the mixture, creating combustion (burning).

spark plug
compressed mixture

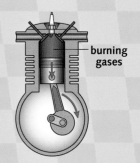

3. POWER STROKE
The burning gases created by combustion push the piston downward. This gives the engine its power.

burning gases

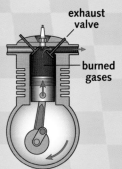

4. EXHAUST STROKE
The piston moves up again and pushes out the burned-out exhaust gases through the exhaust valve.

exhaust valve
burned gases

The Hot One and the Edsel

Meanwhile, Chevrolet was creating a string of classic cars. The division re-designed its Bel Air model for 1955. The new car featured a two-color paint job with lots of shiny chrome trim. The 1955 Bel Air also came with a power-ful new engine, the small-block V8. The car was fast and fun to drive. The engine earned the nickname the Hot One, and the Bel Air was a hot seller.

Chevrolet continued to mix style and speed in the years that followed. The elegant 1957 Bel Air is a great example. From its nifty hood ornaments to its graceful tail fins, the 1957 Chevy is one of the most beautiful cars ever made.

Ford's Fairlane models sold well during these years. One of Ford's most unusual models of the time was the 1957 Fairlane 500 Skyliner. It fea-tured a mechanical roof. With the push of a button, the roof slid into the car's trunk. The Skyliner was beautiful but expensive. And its complicated roof tended to break down.

The Skyliner's troubles were not the only problem at Ford. The company launched its Edsel line of cars in 1957. They were supposed to be on the cut-ting edge of car design. But most peo-ple thought they looked awful. The Edsel's unusual oval-shaped grille was-n't popular. Many people said it looked like a toilet seat or a horse col-lar. Few people bought them. The Edsel line lasted just three years. Ford lost about $400 million on the project.

The 1957 Ford Edsel looked much different than the cars that came before it. Unfortunately, car buyers didn't like the new look.

Among U.S. automakers, Cadillac has always been a leader when it comes to style and luxury. The amazingly long and low Eldorado *(below)* has become a symbol of the outrageous style of 1950s American cars.

Space-Age Cars

The first spaceflights took place in the 1950s. These years are known as the space age. U.S. automobiles reflected the times. Over the years, tail fins were made bigger, so cars looked almost like rocket ships. The 1959 Cadillac Eldorado was the ultimate example of this. It was very long and low. It featured tall, sharp tail fins. Its rear taillights looked like the glow of rocket engines. Other "finny" machines of that year included the Dodge Custom Royal Lancer, the Plymouth Fury, and the massive, chrome-heavy Pontiac Bonneville.

By the early years of the 1960s, American tastes were starting to change. Big cars were still popular in the United States. But as the decade went on, bigger wouldn't always be better.

Pontiac's answer to the Cadillac Eldorado was the 1959 Bonneville. Like the Eldorado, the Bonneville featured tail fins and other rocket ship–inspired details.

Small Is Beautiful

By the mid-1960s, a new generation of young people was reaching driving age. These drivers were looking for something new and exciting. A lot of them went for cars that were different than the usual big U.S. cars. Small cars—called compacts or subcompacts—rose in popularity.

The most popular subcompact car of all time is the Volkswagen Beetle.

The cars were made in Germany and imported to the United States. For many young people, the cute, cheap, and reliable Bug was a nice change. The Volkswagen was by far the best-selling imported car of the 1960s. The Big Three responded by building their own compact cars. They included the Ford Falcon, the Chevrolet Corvair, and the Dodge Lancer.

The Volkswagen Beetle was designed in Germany before World War II.

Mustangs and Muscle

Not everyone was interested in cute cars. U.S. automakers saw that young people wanted cool cars too. In 1964 Ford introduced one of the coolest cars of all time—the Mustang. The snazzy, compact coupe was an instant hit with auto buyers. The Mustang was also affordable. Ford sold more than 400,000 of its "pony cars" during its first model year.

Yet some car buyers wanted more than just looks. Speed and performance were important. A few months after the Mustang first appeared, Pontiac came out with a car that caused a sensation in the auto industry—the GTO.

The powerful 1964 Pontiac GTO coupe helped start the muscle car era.

What Does GTO Stand For?

Pontiac borrowed the name GTO from an Italian high-performance sports car, the Ferrari 250 GTO. *GTO* stands for *Gran Turismo Omologato*. Gran Turismo is a kind of road race. Omologato means "sanctioned, or approved, for racing."

American Motors

From the 1950s through the 1980s, the American Motors Corporation (AMC) was the smallest U.S. automaker. AMC was created in 1954 when two companies, Hudson and Nash-Kelvinator, joined together. The company produced cars in the small city of Kenosha, Wisconsin. AMC produced many popular cars, including the Javelin, the AMX *(below)*, the Gremlin, and the Pacer. AMC fans highly prize these cars. But the AMC vehicles that sold best were its Jeeps—the Jeep Wrangler, the Jeep Cherokee, and the Jeep Grand Cherokee. Chrysler bought AMC in 1987, and the company was shut down a year later. But Chrysler continues to produce the Jeep line in huge numbers.

The GTO was a midsize car. It was bigger than a compact but smaller than a big luxury sedan. Sleek and sporty, the GTO looked great. But that wasn't all. The GTO's powerful engine made it one of the fastest cars on the road. The GTO was a smash hit. It started a whole new era in automobile history—the muscle car era.

Soon every other U.S. automaker was scrambling to come up with its own version of the GTO. While Oldsmobile unleashed its powerful 4-4-2, Buick set loose its brand-new Gran Sport. By 1967 Chrysler had introduced the Plymouth GTX and the Dodge R/T. The following year, Ford began to offer huge engines as options on its Mustang. Even tiny American Motors Corporation offered a muscle car, the small and powerful AMX. These cars had tire-burning speed. All have become collector's items for classic car lovers.

Although the first
Oldsmobile 4-4-2s came out
in 1964, the car continued to
be popular among car fans
for many years. This is the
1966 version.

As the 1960s raced to the finish line, U.S. automakers were working day and night to create faster and more powerful engines. The muscle car years produced some of the great classic cars of all time. They include the striking and powerful 1970 Chevrolet Chevelle. The racetrack-ready 1970 Plymouth Road Runner Superbird could reach speeds close to 200 miles (322 km) per hour.

This 1970 Plymouth Road Runner Superbird was built to rule the speedways of NASCAR®.

But the muscle car craze couldn't last forever. Young thrill seekers and high-performance cars were a dangerous mix. Some people couldn't handle such powerful cars. Many deadly accidents occurred. And those big engines tended to suck up gas and belch out gobs of exhaust. By the early 1970s, the U.S. government was becoming more and more concerned about air pollution and auto safety. Gasoline shortages and rising gas prices didn't help either. By the mid-1970s, the muscle car was all but dead. Only a handful of high-performance cars were still being built.

The Late 1970s: Dog Days of the U.S. Car Industry

The U.S. economy was going through tough times by the mid-1970s. So was the U.S. auto industry. GM, Ford, and Chrysler were struggling to design and build cars that captured the public's imagination. Meanwhile, they were facing tough competition from foreign carmakers, such as Honda, Toyota, Datsun, and Volkswagen.

Japanese automakers specialized in compact and subcompact cars, such as the Honda Civic and the Toyota Celica. These cars were cheap, reliable, and fuel efficient. U.S. car buyers snapped them up by the tens of thousands.

At the same time, GM, Ford, and Chrysler were offering cars of poor quality. Chevrolet's subcompact, the Vega, was unreliable. Ford's Pinto sub-compact was downright dangerous. Many Pintos burst into flames after being hit from behind. U.S. cars developed a poor reputation in the 1970s.

But a few classics did come out of the decade. The Pontiac Firebird and Chevrolet Camaro are popular collector cars. The Chevrolet Monte Carlo of the late 1970s was a sporty, midsize luxury car. The unusual, bubble-shaped

With cool bucket seats and a huge engine under the hood, the 1971 Pontiac Firebird is one of the few classic cars to come out of the early 1970s.

This 1990 Corvette ZR1 is one of the many redesigns of the classic Corvette.

AMC Pacer has also become a classic. But the 1970s weren't the best era for U.S. automobiles.

Modern-Day and Future Classic Cars

What modern cars will become classics? It's hard to know for sure. But newer versions of old classics remain popular. For example, the Ford Mustang and Chevrolet Corvette have had many redesigns over the years. Newer versions of these cars still sell well. The redesigned 2005 Mustang has been a big hit.

Meanwhile, Chrysler has created a series of new and exciting cars in recent years. The Chrysler PT Cruiser is a modern car that has a classic look. Its front grille and rounded shape make it look like a car from the past. Chrysler's 300 series are updated versions of the C-300. They are luxury sedans with powerful engines. Automakers of modern times look to cars of the past to make great cars for the future.

The PT Cruiser may have a classic look, but it's completely modern under the hood. The 2.4-liter turbocharged engine produces about 230 horsepower.

Chapter Two

Classic Car Culture

The United States is home to thousands of classic car lovers. Some of these people own and collect classic cars. Others enjoy them in different ways. Some read books and magazines about their favorite cars and go to auto shows to see them.

Classic Car Collecting

A car collector might be a wealthy person who owns dozens of classic cars. A person with a big car collection probably has a huge storage garage. Some employ mechanics to keep their cars in top shape. These collectors might even loan their cars to museums so other people can see them up close.

Most collectors own just one or a few special vehicles. Classic cars are their favorite hobby. Their cars are their most prized possessions.

Some collectors buy cars that are already in good shape. They want to enjoy driving and looking at these amazing vehicles.

But many other collectors enjoy working on their cars. They buy vehicles that are in bad shape and fix them up. Some people can make a liv-ing fixing up old cars. The classic car business can be very profitable. But it takes a lot of skill and hard work to do the job right.

Customizing and restoring are the two most popular ways to fix up classic cars. Restoring is taking an old car and making it look brand new. Customizing

Car collectors often assemble a wide variety of cars. The cars shown here include a 1967 Corvette C2 427 *(bottom left)*, two late 1960s Ford Shelby Mustangs *(top left and far right)*, and a 1960s Plymouth GTX *(top right)*.

is adding unique parts to make the car one of a kind.

Customizing

People customize cars in many different ways. For example, a person might cut a hole in the hood to make room for a supercharger, or blower. This device sits on top of the engine and forces air into the engine, adding an extra boost of horsepower. A big, shiny, chrome blower also looks really cool sticking out of a car's hood.

Custom exhaust pipes called headers add power to engines and look appealing. Adding a bigger carburetor is another popular way to go. (A carburetor mixes fuel and air for combustion.) And of course, adding a more powerful engine is always an option.

Performance can be boosted in other ways. Adding extra-wide tires to the back wheels gives a car more grip. Extra grip helps a car get off the starting line faster in races. And those fat tires look great too.

When it comes to customizing a car's look, chrome is the way to go. Chrome engine parts, chrome exhaust pipes, and chrome wheels are the most popular options. People also jazz up their cars' interiors with fuzzy seats or loud stereos.

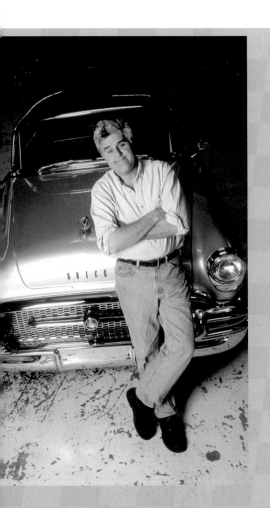

Jay Leno, Car Collector

Jay Leno (born 1950), host of NBC's *The Tonight Show with Jay Leno*, is a big car collector. Leno owns more than 100 cars and motorcycles. He keeps his vehicles in a huge warehouse and has a team of people to keep his cars in tip-top shape.

His collection includes high-priced super sports cars such as Italian Lamborghinis and powerful U.S. muscle cars. He also owns a few Stanley Steamers. These unusual cars from the early 1900s were powered by steam engines. Leno often drives cars from his collection to and from *The Tonight Show*'s studios.

People use their imaginations to come up with new and better customizations for their classic cars. But regardless of the type of work being done, customization is always a hands-on job.

Restoring a classic car is painstaking work. After the car has been repainted, the chrome trim and other features must be replaced.

Hundreds of companies around the United States make custom parts for all sorts of cars.

The most popular way to customize a car is to give it a fancy paint job. Custom paint jobs allow for fun designs such as flames, racing stripes, and even illustrations. Custom painting gives a car a one-of-kind look.

Restoring

Many collectors enjoy restoring classic cars. The idea is to make the car look exactly the way it did when it came from the factory. Some collectors value cars that look brand new from bumper to bumper.

Restoring an old car takes hard work and an eye for detail. It usually means stripping the car down to the bare body and then removing all the paint. After the paint is gone, the restorer will fill any dents, bumps, or scratches. The idea is to make the body look as good as new. Once the body is finished, the restorer adds multiple coats of paint.

When the painting is done, the restorer begins to put the car back together. The restorer can use the car's original parts or buy new ones. Many companies make parts for older vehicles.

After the car is put back together, it's time to start it up and take it for a drive. Or the owner might show it

off at the local car club or at a car show.

Classic Car Clubs and Shows

The United States is home to hundreds of car clubs. These clubs are great places for people to get together and talk about their favorite cars. Club members show off their vehicles and share tips for customizing and restoring. They may even sell their vehicles to one another. Many clubs produce newsletters that

Clubs are great places for classic car lovers to get together. They show off their vehicles or talk about upcoming events, such as car shows.

29

Car shows are held outdoors in fields and parking lots and indoors in convention centers and other large buildings. The only requirement for a car show is lots of space for all the people and vehicles.

describe what members are up to and upcoming events. Car clubs often organize car shows.

Car shows are the best places to see lots of classic cars. Every year, car collectors hold shows all over the country. They are the most popular way for people to show off their cars. They're also great places to talk about cars with other car fans.

Car shows are usually held in a big place, such as a fairground or a big parking lot. Car owners line up their cars in rows. They usually open the hood to show off the engine. Collectors and fans wander around, checking out the cars. Sometimes shows feature experts or famous people, such as car designers or race car drivers. Most shows have auctions, where people can buy and sell their cars. Car shows are a fun way to spend a day and to learn about cars and collectors. But cars don't just sit still at shows. Many events feature races and cruises too.

Races and Cruises

Car show races take place on tracks. Drivers can go fast without getting into trouble.

National Street Rod Association

The National Street Rod Association (NSRA) is one of the biggest car organizations in the United States. The NSRA hosts some of the largest car events in the country. These events feature games, music, cruises, and, of course, hundreds of cars. Classic car collectors from around the country bring their cars to these events. The NSRA also publishes its own monthly magazine, *StreetScene*.

Classic cars that have been nicely restored are often put on public display. The Automotive Hall of Fame in Dearborn, Michigan, showcases this 1956 Cadillac Sedan DeVille.

A 1968 Plymouth GTX leaves
other cars in its dust at a
car show drag race in
Pomona, California.

Drag racing is the most popular kind of automobile racing. In a drag race, two cars compete on a short, straight track. Pure speed is the goal. The car that can accelerate the fastest is the winner.

Drag races are fun to attend. The smell of burning rubber, the roar of engines, and the screaming crowds are really exciting. And drag racing is fairly safe too. Since the cars drive straight for a short distance, there is little danger of crashing.

Nicknames

Car enthusiasts often refer to the Ford Motor Company as the Blue Oval, after the company's trademark emblem. Chevrolet's cross-shaped emblem is known as the bow tie. Chrysler's vehicles are often called Mopar products, after the company's parts division. *Mopar* is short for "*motor parts.*"

Cruising is another amusing car activity. Most car shows feature cruises. These events usually take place in the evening. A cruise is like a car parade. It's a terrific way to show off your vehicle. Owners drive down a street or highway, one after the other, forming a long line of cars. People stop along the side of the road to watch these amazing machines roll past.

Classic car cruises allow people to see these impressive machines in action.

Young people can find lots of ways to enjoy classic cars. One way is by purchasing collectibles. Classic car collectibles include die-cast metal cars. Companies such as Ertl, GMP Diecast, and ExactDetail make dozens of die-cast metal model cars. They look very realistic and are made in a variety of sizes.

Another popular way to enjoy classic cars is by building models of them. Revell, AMT, and Ertl make excellent plastic model kits. Modelers can make realistic models of their favorite cars. They can paint them any color they want. A skilled painter can even add flames, illustrations, and custom racing stripes.

Plastic models are popular with car enthusiasts of all ages. Revell is one of several companies that make realistic models of classic cars.

Classic Car Media: Magazines and TV Shows

Classic car fans have many ways to keep on top of the latest car activities and trends. Magazines and TV shows are two of the best ways to learn about and enjoy classic cars.

Car magazines include *Hemmings Classic Car, Hemmings Motor News, Classic Car, Hot Rod,* and *Car Craft*.

These magazines feature articles about classic cars and car collectors. They also have the latest news about car shows.

TV shows about cars are all the rage. Cable networks such as MTV, the Discovery Channel, Speed Channel, the History Channel, and TLC run shows about cars. Speed Channel's *Car Crazy* is all about people who love cars. *My Classic Car*, also on Speed Channel, visits car shows and events all around the country.

Other car shows feature makeovers. Mechanics take old cars and customize them in crazy ways. For example, MTV's popular show *Pimp My Ride* takes old, beat-up cars and turns them into incredible custom machines. *Overhaulin'*, on TLC network, does the same thing. What makes *Overhaulin'* fun is that the owner doesn't know that the car is getting a makeover. People are pretty excited when they see what happens to their old, beat-up vehicles!

Lee Iacocca

Lee Iacocca *(right)* took over at Chrysler in 1978. The company was in serious financial trouble and in danger of going out of business. Iacocca helped turn Chrysler around by introducing some very successful cars, including the minivan. His success made him a popular celebrity. His autobiography, *Iacocca: An Autobiography*, was a huge best seller in the 1980s.

Classic Car Restoration

In the early 2000s, Mike and June Key decided to restore a 1966 Ford Mustang. The heap was in a bad state. It was rusted throughout, and the interior was in ruins.

Mike and June stripped the car themselves. What was left was just the chassis and the front and rear suspension. Their next step was to scrape and weld the car's underside and the area where a new engine would go. Mike replaced the dash and other worn-out parts. He then painted all these parts Satin Black. The couple got help from some expert friends. One fixed the badly rusted metal parts of the car's exterior. Another primed and painted the exterior bright red.

June got back into the act when the windows, doors, and carpets were installed. Together, she and Mike struggled through the job of recovering the front and back seats, also in bright red.

By 2005 the car was ready for driving. Mike says it's very close to how the car came out of the factory in 1966. Sweet!

1. The rusted-out 1966 Ford Mustang arrived at the house of Mike and June Key. Their first idea was to restore the car so it could be just an additional vehicle for the family, not a show car. But after they got going on the restoration, they realized that, no matter what, the project would be a lot of work. They decided to restore the car to its original look.

2. Preparing the car's body for painting took a huge amount of time. Mike's friend Paul Wayling *(below)* scraped and sanded the larger sections of the metal exterior that had been bent or badly rusted. Mike helped by taking care of smaller dings.

3. A crack in the chassis meant the area needed to be cleaned up and sanded before welding could take place.

4. Mike completely cleaned out and repainted the engine bay. A beautiful cleaned-up engine was ready to put inside.

5. A special room was needed to completely spray the body with its new bright red color.

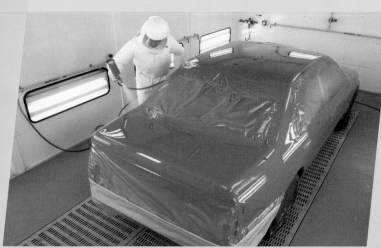

6. June Key worked hard to get the upholstery just right on the bucket seats *(inset)*. Two years after they started, the Keys had a fully restored and fun-to-drive Mustang.

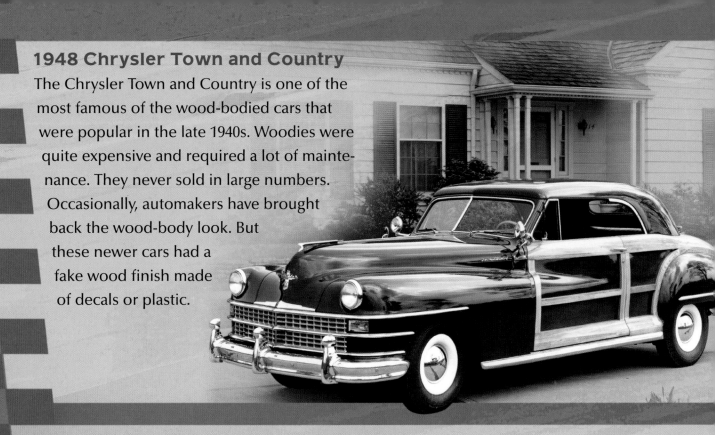

1948 Chrysler Town and Country

The Chrysler Town and Country is one of the most famous of the wood-bodied cars that were popular in the late 1940s. Woodies were quite expensive and required a lot of maintenance. They never sold in large numbers. Occasionally, automakers have brought back the wood-body look. But these newer cars had a fake wood finish made of decals or plastic.

1948 Tucker Torpedo

The short-lived Tucker Torpedo was years ahead of its time. The car's new ideas included a sturdy passenger area and padded interior for safety. The Torpedo could accelerate from 0 to 60 miles (96 km) per hour in just 10 seconds with a top speed of 120 miles (193 km) per hour. Legal problems ruined Preston Tucker's business before it could get off the ground, however. Tucker's story is told in the 1988 movie, *Tucker: The Man and His Dream*, starring Jeff Bridges.

1949 Buick Roadmaster

The Roadmaster was part of the first wave of all-new post-World War II cars from GM. Its smooth front end and fastback rear made it a popular choice. The Roadmaster featured an in-line, or straight, eight-cylinder engine. A straight, eight-cylinder engine has its eight cylinders arranged in a single row. Roadmaster options included the Dynaflow automatic transmission. An automatic transmission changes gears automatically.

1949 Ford

The simple but attractive 1949 Ford was launched in June 1948. Its mix of nice looks and a low price made it an instant hit, and Ford sold more than a million of them. Unlike pre-World War II cars, the 1949 Ford had flat sides. This is known as a slab-sided look.

Volkswagen Beetle

The Beetle was built by order of German Nazi leader Adolf Hitler and designed by Ferdinand Porsche. Hitler wanted a car that was small, efficient, and easy to build. The result was one of the most popular cars of all time—the bug-shaped, rear-engine Beetle. Volkswagen produced Beetles in various forms from 1938 to 2003. In 1998 Volkswagen unveiled a new, totally redesigned Beetle. Car fans bought them in droves.

1955 Ford Thunderbird

The Thunderbird was Ford's answer to the Chevrolet Corvette. The Thunderbird actually sold better than its rival. This stylish and glamorous coupe was popular with movie stars and other famous people. Ford even offered the unusual color option of pink. In the 1960s, Ford redesigned the car from a small sporty coupe into a big, spacious luxury car.

1957 Cadillac Eldorado

The 1957 Caddy was the ultimate space-age car. Its tall, pointy tail fins looked like the fins on a rocket ship. The car's taillights looked like roaring rocket engines. The car has become one of the great classic U.S. cars and a popular collector's item.

1957 Chevrolet Bel Air

The ultimate classic car combined great looks and great performance. The 1957 Bel Air is by far the most popular classic U.S. car. These cars were not only beautiful. They were one of the fastest cars produced in the 1950s. Many were equipped with fuel-injected engines. (Fuel injection delivers the air-fuel mixture to the cylinder with a pump instead of the usual carburetor.)

1959 Ford Edsel

Is this car ugly? Most Americans thought so when the Edsel came out for the 1959 model year. Ford had spent hundreds of millions of dollars developing its new line of Edsels. The cars were supposed to be the cutting edge of design. Instead, they were a massive flop.

1962 Chevrolet Corvair

The Corvair was GM's answer to the growing popularity of the Volkswagen Beetle. Like the Beetle, it featured an air-cooled (instead of the usual liquid-cooled) engine mounted in the rear. The sporty machine looked good but had many mechanical and safety problems. The car did not sell very well, and Chevrolet dropped the model in 1969.

1964 Chevrolet Corvette Sting Ray

Harley Earl retired in 1959. His replacement, Bill Mitchell, brought a new look to GM's cars. One of his greatest cars was the redesigned Corvette. The Sting Ray was a brilliant blend of great looks and horsepower. Its new design featured two rear windows. It could be purchased with a powerful V8 engine that made the Corvette one of the fastest cars on the road.

1965 Ford Mustang

The Mustang made a huge splash when it arrived on the scene. The car had the perfect combination of great looks and a low price. Ford sold more than 400,000 for the 1965 model year. The original Mustang has been redesigned several times and continues to sell in huge numbers.

1975 AMC Pacer

American Motors Company launched the Pacer for the 1975 model year. The car created a splash with its funky look. The bubble-shaped car was nearly as wide as it was long. This made it very roomy inside and a good family car. It also got better gas mileage than the usual big family cars. But not everyone liked the Pacer's unusual look, and the car was not very successful.

1982 Chevrolet Camaro

The first Camaros came out in 1967. They were Chevrolet's answer to the small and popular Mustang. The 1982 model was the first major redesign of this successful car. It was a big change from the rounded shape of the earlier Camaros. But like the older versions, they were still fast and sporty.

2001 Chrysler PT Cruiser

Chrysler introduced the sporty PT Cruiser for the 2001 model year. It quickly became the company's top-selling model. U.S. car buyers were thrilled with the car's classic look. The Cruiser reminded many people of cars of the 1930s and 1940s. The PT Cruiser remains a big seller, and many people think it will become a popular collector's item.

2005 Ford Mustang

The latest Mustang model has all the makings of a classic. The car's overall look is an updated version of the early Mustangs of the mid-1960s. The car's grille and taillights bring to mind the classic Mustangs of old.

Glossary

accelerate: to go from a stop or from a slow speed to a fast speed

coupe: a two-door car that usually seats just two people

customizing: taking an old car and making it into a one-of-a-kind vehicle by adding special parts, a unique paint job, and so on

drag racing: a racing competition in which two cars race side by side. Most drag races run a quarter mile.

fastback: a car design that features a roof that slopes down to the rear end

fuel injection: in an internal-combustion engine, a system that injects fuel into the cylinders with a pump instead of with a carburetor

headers: high-performance exhaust pipes. Headers are designed to add horsepower by helping the engine breathe easier.

horsepower: a unit used to measure the amount of power an engine can produce. Horsepower was originally measured as the amount of work a certain kind of horse could do in a day.

model year: the particular year that a car is produced. For U.S. automakers, the model year begins a few months before the calendar year. For example, cars for the 1968 model year became widely available in late 1967.

option: a part or feature of a car, such as a bigger engine, that a buyer can choose to have installed for additional cost

restoring: taking an old car and making it look brand new. Most restorers try to make their cars look just like they did when they came from the factory.

sedan: a car with a solid roof that is designed to seat four or more people. Most sedans have four doors.

standard: a feature on a car for which the customer does not need to pay extra

supercharger: a device that forces compressed air into an engine's combustion chamber, creating more horsepower

Selected Bibliography

DeLorenzo, Matt. *American Cars: Past to Present*. New York: Barnes and Noble Books, 2004.

Lewis, Lucinda. *Roadside America: The Automobile and the American Dream*. New York: Harry N. Abrams, 2000.

Mueller, Mike. *Essential Musclecars*. Saint Paul: Motorbooks International, 2004.

____. *Muscle Car Icons: Ford, Chevy & Chrysler*. Saint Paul: Crestline, 2003.

Nicholls, Richard. *American Classic Cars*. New York: Barnes and Noble Books, 2002.

Willson, Quentin. *Cars: A Celebration*. New York: Dorling Kindersley, 2001.

Mueller, Mike. *The Corvette*. Saint Paul: Crestline, 2003.

Newhardt, David. *The Mustang*. Saint Paul: Crestline, 2003.

Zuehlke, Jeffrey. *Muscle Cars*. Minneapolis: Lerner Publications Company, 2007.

Further Reading

Leffingwell, Randy. *Hot Wheels: 35 Years of Speed, Power, Performance, and Attitude*. Osceola, WI: Motorbooks International, 2003.

Websites

Hemmings Motor News
http://www.hemmings.com
Hemmings Motor News is a top resource for any car fan. The company publishes several popular magazines. Its website features names and addresses of auto clubs and auto museums from all 50 states and much more.

Official Harley Earl Website
http://www.carofthecentury.com/
Learn more about GM design wizard Harley Earl from his official website. The site features information on Earl's life, his impact on the automobile industry, and photos of his most famous cars.

Index

About the Author

Jeffrey Zuehlke is a writer and editor. He has written more than a dozen nonfiction books for children. He lives in Minneapolis.

About the Consultant

Jan Lahtonen is a safety engineer, auto mechanic, and lifelong automobile enthusiast.

Photo Acknowledgments

The images in this book are used with the permission of: Copyright 2006 GM Corp. Used with permission, GM Media Archive, pp. 4–5, 10, 14, 15, 17, 21, 39 (top), 41 (bottom), 42 (bottom), 44 (bottom); © Ralph Morse/Time & Life Pictures/Getty Images, pp. 6–7 (top); Courtesy Of: Daimler Chrysler Historical Collection. Copyright DaimlerChrysler Corporation. Used with permission, pp. 6 (bottom), 7, 11, 20, 24–25, 38 (top), 44 (top); Ford Motor Company, pp. 8, 39 (bottom), 45 (bottom); © Mike Mueller, p. 9; © Laura Westlund /Independent Picture Service, p. 12; © M. McKeown/Express/Hulton Archive/Getty Images, p. 13; © Hulton Archive/Getty Images, p. 16; © G. Paulina/ TRANSTOCK, p. 18; © Jerry Heasley, p. 19; © Andrew Sacks/Time & Life Pictures/Getty Images, p. 22; © J. Flores Cobleigh/ TRANSTOCK, p. 23; © Ronald Martinez/ Allsport/Getty Images, p. 25; © B. Jaynes/ TRANSTOCK, p. 26; © Strauss/Curtis/ CORBIS, p. 27; © Mike Key, pp. 28, 36 (both), 37 (top), 37 (right), 37 (bottom), 37 (bottom inset), 41 (top), 42 (top); © Ethan Miller/ Getty Images, p. 29; © Bill Pugliano/Getty Images, p. 30; © Richard Cummins/CORBIS, p. 31; © Mirek Towski/Time & Life Pictures/ Getty Images, p. 32; © Todd Strand/ Independent Picture Service, pp. 33, 34; © Ted Thai/Time & Life Pictures/Getty Images, p. 35; © Roger Ball/CORBIS, p. 37 (left); © CORBIS, p. 38 (bottom); © Bettmann/ CORBIS, p. 40 (top); © Tom Brakefield/ SuperStock, p. 40 (bottom); © Tom Brakefield/ CORBIS, p. 43 (top); Photo courtesy of the National Automobile Museum (The Harrah Collection), Reno, Nevada, p. 43 (bottom); © G. Spangenberg/TRANSTOCK, p. 45 (top).

Front Cover: © Sam Lund/Independent Picture Service.